# The Mystery
## of the
# Loch Ness Monster

# The Mystery
## of the
# Loch Ness Monster

## BY JEANNE BENDICK

MᴄGʀᴀᴡ-Hɪʟʟ Bᴏᴏᴋ Cᴏᴍᴘᴀɴʏ

w York   St. Louis   San Francisco   Auckland   Düsseldorf   Johannesburg
uala Lumpur   London   Mexico   Montreal   New Delhi   Panama   Paris
São Paulo   Singapore   Sydney   Tokyo   Toronto

# To Bob

Thanks!
To Dr. Robert Rines and the Academy of
Applied Science, and to the Society For the
Investigation of the Unexplained for the gen-
erous use of their library.

Library of Congress Cataloging in Publication Data
Bendick, Jeanne.
    The mystery of the Loch Ness Monster.

    Bibliography: p.
    Includes index.
    SUMMARY: Examines the mystery of the Loch Ness
monster by reviewing its history, the geography of the lake,
maps, photographs, and sketches.
        1. Loch Ness monster—Juvenile literature. [1. Loch
Ness     monster.     2.     Monsters]     I. Title.
QL89.2.L6B46        001.9'44        76–18083
ISBN 0–07–004496–1
ISBN 0–07–004497–X lib. bdg.

2345 BPBP 78987

# Contents

# 1
# *The Monster Lives Here*

**I**N THE MISTY HILLS of northern Scotland there is a deep, dark lake called Loch Ness. Something mysterious seems to live in that lonely lake. People call it the Loch Ness Monster.

Thousands of people have reported seeing the Monster, but nobody has seen *all* of it.

Nobody has taken a clear picture of it.

Nobody has caught a monster or touched it.

Nobody has ever found the bones of a dead one.

Nobody really knows what it is.

But whatever the Monster is, Loch Ness has been its home for a long, long time.

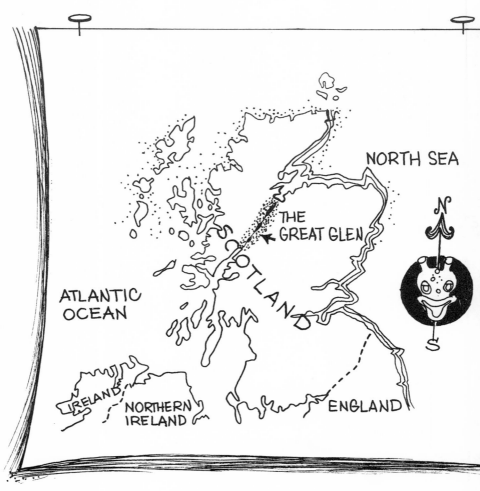

Loch Ness is in the Great Glen of Scotland—a deep split in the earth's surface that runs all the way across the Highlands of northern Scotland from the Atlantic Ocean to the North Sea. There aren't many sunny days there. Sometimes the wind from the sea whistles through the Glen, whipping up the cold, dark water.

The Great Glen is a fault—a weak place in the earth's crust along which earthquakes happen. It was formed about 300 million years ago when there were many violent earthquakes on earth. The plates that make up the earth's crust shifted. The continents began to move apart, and the ground split open. The sea flowed in. For millions of years the Great Glen was an arm of the ocean. Dinosaurs, plesiosaurs, and other huge prehistoric animals lived there then. Their bones have been found in many places in the British Isles.

## HOW LOCHS WERE FORMED

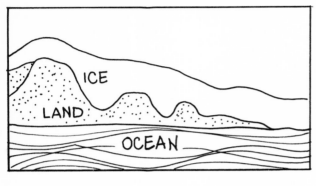

1. *A sheet of ice covered land and water.*

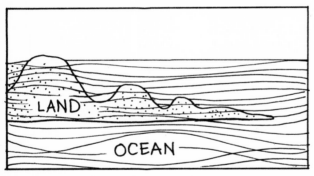

2. *As the ice melted the water level rose and the ocean covered the land in many places.*

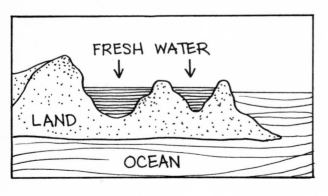

3. *Finally, the land rose in some places and the water in the valleys was locked in. Over a long time, it became fresh.*

About 60 million years ago the climate on earth began to get colder. The northern seas froze and the ice began to spread. About 3 million years ago a sheet of ice, almost a mile thick in some places, had covered a lot of the Northern Hemisphere.

The ice ground up the soil and moved huge rocks around. It pushed rocks and soil ahead of it. It dug great holes in the earth's surface and made deep places like the Great Glen even deeper.

Then slowly, about 18,000 years ago, the climate changed again and the ice began to melt. With all that ice melting into water, the levels of the oceans rose. The sea flowed over the land and into the enormous holes the ice had dug.

The descendants of many of the animals that had fled south so long before to escape the ice began to come north again.

Ten or 15,000 years ago the weight of all the ground-up rocks and soil began to change the shape of the Great Glen. In some places the earth's crust sank. In others it buckled and rose. When that happened the deep pools of sea water in the Great Glen were cut off from the ocean and locked in. Once they were cut off, those pools were fed only by streams and springs from the mountains, and gradually the water changed from salty to fresh. That's how Loch Ness and the other deep, inland lakes around the northern part of the earth were formed.

Loch Ness is the biggest freshwater lake in Britain. It's about 24 miles (38.4 kilometers) long and about a mile and a half (2.4 kilometers) wide. In most places it's about 450 feet (137 meters) deep. But in some places it is more than 900 feet (274 meters) deep. There may be even deeper places, but this lake is hard to explore.

The water in the loch is dark brown, like coffee. That's because the streams and rivers that empty into Loch Ness flow through ancient bogs and swamps, bringing in tons of decayed plant stuff called *peat*. The peat hangs thick in the water. About 50 feet (15.2 meters) down the water is so thick and dark that you can't see anything in any direction. The few divers who have gone down into the loch say that you can't even tell which way is up and which way is down. Most of them never go down again.

People don't swim much in Loch Ness, especially the people whose families have always lived there. For many centuries there have been stories of strange animals living in the loch and in other lakes nearby. In some places children are still forbidden to swim in the lakes for fear that the "water beasties" might get them.

You probably wouldn't want to go swimming in most of Loch Ness anyway, even if you weren't afraid of meeting a monster. The water is very cold all year round. The average temperature is about 42°F (5°C). And there are dangerous currents under the surface. That's because the sides of the loch are like cliffs, dropping sharply down to the bottom. In the part of the loch called Urquhart Bay, some people think there are underwater caves in the sides.

Also in Urquhart Bay there are long hills and deep valleys on the bottom. Urquhart Bay is where the

*Scottish Tourist Board*

Monster is most often reported. On a cliff overlooking the bay stands a huge, ruined castle.

No green plants grow in most of the loch because the peat keeps sunlight out. The bottom of the loch is covered with a thick layer of peat that has settled there over thousands of years.

But the peat doesn't pollute the lake even though it turns the water brown. The water is fresh and healthy for animals. Loch Ness is a famous fishing place. A lot of very big salmon live there—millions of them. There are very big trout, too, and in the deepest places a relative of the trout and salmon called Arctic char. All these fish are predators. They eat smaller fishes, tiny water animals and insects. There is a large population of eels in the lake. Many of them are very big. Otters live there, and some of those are very large as well.

All around Loch Ness there are mountains and thick woods, where big deer live, and eagles, and even some wildcats.

Closer to the loch, on hills sloping down toward the water, there are some farms. You can see the loch from

*General Wade supervising the building of his road. The bridge in the background is still part of it.*

some of the farms. You can see what's swimming in the loch, too.

For a long time it was hard to get around the loch. The only real road was an old military supply road called General Wade's Road. General Wade's Road was built on the south side of the loch during a war in 1715. The men who built the road told stories of two huge creatures they saw, several times, in the loch—creatures "as big as whales."

General Wade's Road is still there. Along the road the trees are thick, the cliffs are steep and rocky, and there is hardly a place to get a clear view of the water. On the north side of the loch there was only an old winding track, running up and down the hills, into the woods and out of them, near the loch and away from it.

But there was a lot of traffic on the loch itself. There are three lakes in the Great Glen—Loch Ness, Loch

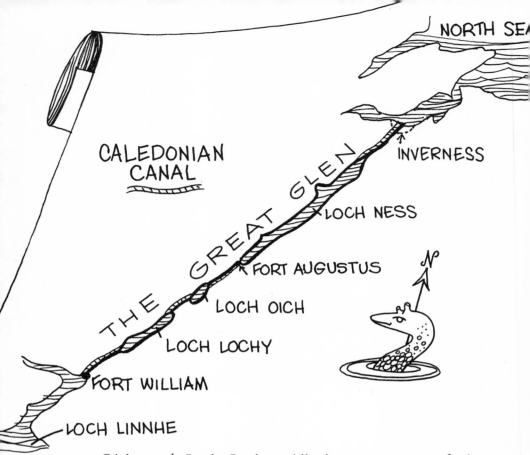

Oich, and Loch Lochy. All three are part of the Caledonian Canal. The canal was built across the Great Glen more than 150 years ago as a shortcut between the Atlantic Ocean and the North Sea. Once the canal was built ships did not have to sail all the way around the dangerous, rocky northern shore of Scotland to get from one sea to the other.

The men who built the canal reported seeing "monster fish." So did crews on canal boats. Many, many boats, big commercial ones and pleasure boats, use the canal. At the North Sea entrance is the city of Inverness. At the other end is Fort William, where the canal empties into Loch Linnhe, a deep, saltwater inlet of the Atlantic Ocean.

*Nothing* can get into Loch Ness from the sea—or out of it, back into the sea—without coming through the locks in the canal. The locks are there because Loch Ness is about 50 feet (15.2 meters) above sea level. Boats coming through the canal must be lifted toward Loch Ness, lock by lock, then lowered, lock by lock, going out.

Between Loch Ness and the North Sea there are seven locks and the shallow River Ness, which runs through the center of Inverness.

Between Loch Ness and the Atlantic Ocean there are seventeen locks. It is almost impossible for anything

*Scottish Tourist Board*

*The River Ness at Inverness.*

bigger than a salmon to pass through the locks without being seen.

So whatever is in Loch Ness (and in Lochs Oich and Lochy, where mysterious creatures have also been reported) has probably been there for thousands of years.

It could not have come in between the time Loch Ness was cut off from the sea ten thousand years ago

*Boats going through a series of locks in the Caledonian Canal. Could a monster come through without being seen?*

and the time the canal was built, connecting Loch Ness to the sea again. And the chances are very small that it could have come in since without being seen.

In 1933 a new road was built along the north side of the loch, from Inverness to Fort William. It was a modern road, built to carry automobiles, trucks, and buses.

Engineers and road crews came in with their machines. They cleared trees. For the first time it was possible to see across the lake from a number of places, and up and down its length.

They blew up rocks and cliffs with dynamite to make a bed for the road. The earth shook. Tons of dirt and huge boulders splashed into the water, stirring things up.

Crews working on the road saw humps and bumps in the loch. They saw mysterious wakes trailing behind unseen, fast-moving "somethings" in the water. Crews on boats saw large objects moving through the water with V-shaped wakes behind them.

There was a lot of coming and going on the new road, and stories began to spread of a very strange creature that lived in the loch—a *huge* creature. In fact, a monster.

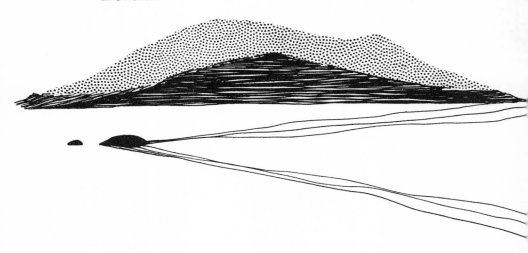

# 2

# *Some History of the Monster Mystery*

AN OLD, OLD LEGEND SAYS that Loch Ness has

> Waves without wind,
> A fish without fin,
> And a floating island.

The waves seem to start up suddenly, somewhere out on the lake. They come even on calm days when there is no wind.

The floating island is a big, dark hump. It rises out of the water, sometimes in one place, sometimes in another. There may be more than one hump.

The fish without fin is the mysterious creature who lives in the loch.

The people who have always lived around Loch Ness accept the fact that the creature is really there.

The first recorded story of it is from A.D. 565, when the Monster was seen at Bonar Narrows, at the head of the loch. The story is in the biography of Saint Columba, a missionary to the Picts, who lived in Scotland at that time. The chapter that tells about Saint Columba and the Monster is called: "Of the driving away of a certain Water Monster, by virtue of Prayer of the Holy Man."

Saint Columba had sent one of his men to swim across the loch to bring back a small boat moored on the other side of the narrows.

". . . But the monster, perceiving the surface of the water disturbed by the swimmer, came up and rushed toward the man, roaring, with an open mouth.

*Statue of Saint Columba at the monastery in Fort Augustus.*

"Then the Blessed Man raised his Holy Hand, invoked the name of God, made the sign of the cross and commanded the terrible monster, saying, 'Thou shalt go no further, nor touch that man; go back with all speed.' And the monster fled, faster than it had come."

For many centuries there have been stories of water bulls and water horses, or "kelpies," in Loch Ness and in the other lochs in the Scotch Highlands. The water horses were supposed to be dangerous. A water horse would come ashore disguised as a beautiful saddle horse and graze quietly until some foolish person mounted it. Then it would gallop into the loch with its rider, who would never be seen again.

All through the years, mixed in with the stories of the water bulls and water horses, there were other stories of a large, eel-like water animal with a humped back and a head like an earless horse.

But huge mysterious water animals weren't reported only in the lochs of Scotland. Since earliest times there have been stories of monster sea animals—people called them sea serpents—in the oceans. Sometimes they appeared close to shore. Sometimes they appeared in the deepest parts of the sea.

Almost 2,500 years ago, in the fourth century B.C., Aristotle, the Greek who was probably the world's first scientific zoologist, described sea serpents . . . ''like beams of wood, black, thick, and round." He also described another monster sea animal that sounds like a giant squid.

When the Romans were in Britain two thousand years ago they said there were sea serpents on the coasts. In the second century they made a mosaic showing how the sea serpents looked.

*The Roman Mosaic called*
*"The Beasts of Nodens."*

For a long time everybody believed in sea serpents.

In the sixteenth century a historian and map maker named Olaus Magnus made a map of the land and oceans of northern Europe.

*Olaus Magnus' map of the North Atlantic.*

Nobody doubted that the animals were there. Some of them *are* real animals that we can recognize today, now that we are more familiar with the way sea animals live and look. There are whales and narwhals, lobsters, flying fish, squid and octopus.

Hans Egede, a Norwegian missionary to Greenland who had a great interest in natural history, described a sea monster he saw from his ship in 1734. He said that it was bigger than the ship itself, with "a Long, pointed Snout, and spouted like a Whale-Fish, great broad Paws and the body seemed covered with shell-work."

*Hans Egede called this*
*"a most dreadful monster."*

*Erik Pontoppidan*

In 1752 the Bishop of Norway, Erik Pontoppidan, published a book called *The Natural History of Norway.*
He claimed that three legendary sea creatures, which he called the mermaid, the kraken, and the sea serpent, or sea orm, were real.

*Mermaids*

*The Kraken attacking a ship.*

*The Sea Orm.*

So far two of these creatures *have* turned out to be real, though we call them by different names.

The mermaid turned out to be a sea mammal called a dugong. It's not a very good-looking mermaid, but passable to a sailor on the deck of a high ship.

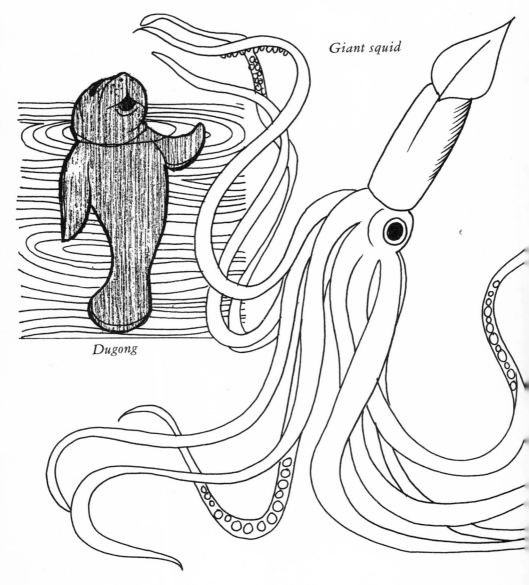

*Giant squid*

*Dugong*

The kraken turned out to be a giant squid. Giant squid have been found with a tentacle spread of 60 feet (18 meters) or more. Some oceanographers say that there may be squid in the deepest parts of the oceans with a spread of 100 feet (30.4 meters).

Pontoppidan was absolutely sure about the sea serpent, too. He said it was a giant snake.

As time went on, people kept reporting sea serpents in different parts of the oceans and scientists kept looking for proof that they really existed. They wanted something they could study and measure and examine.

In 1808 a carcass was found on Stronsa Island, one of the Orkney Islands of Scotland. It was measured by some local people and described as being 55 feet (16.7 meters) long with a mane on a long neck, a tail like a lizard, a small head with a hairy crest, and six "wings."

Because winter was coming and the weather was bad and stormy, it was quite a while before any scientists had a chance to examine the remains. When they did, some declared that the body was that of a true sea monster. They even proposed a scientific name for it—*Halsydrus pontoppidani*, because it seemed to be the beast Pontoppidan had described.

In science, giving a species a scientific name is an important event. It means that scientists have recognized a new species—a new kind of plant or animal.

But on further examination the Stronsa monster turned out to be the rotting remains of a huge basking shark and the scientists who had declared it to be a new species were humiliated. Scientists take making a mistake just as hard as anyone else.

In the summer of 1817 there was more sea-monster excitement. Hundreds of people reported seeing an enormous sea snake with a humped back in Gloucester Harbor, in Massachusetts. It was sighted many times during that summer.

The Linnean Society of New England, a group of distinguished scientists, had a theory that the great sea snake had come in to shore to lay its eggs as sea turtles do. They began a search for sea-serpent eggs.

*Carolus Linnaeus was a Swedish naturalist who established the scientific method we use for naming plants and animals.*

*The Glouscester Monster.*

Then one day some boys found a large, black snake on the beach. It had three humps on its back. The scientists of the Linnean Society decided that it was a baby sea serpent. They published an article about it in their journal, along with pictures.

A French naturalist who saw the pictures pointed out that the baby sea serpent looked like an ordinary big snake with some odd growths on its back. When it was examined more carefully, that was just what the "serpent" turned out to be. Again a group of scientists had been humiliated and embarrassed over a sea-serpent controversy.

The group never tackled the subject again in spite of the fact that the mistake over the "baby sea serpent" did *not* disprove the presence of the big sea serpent that so many people had seen all summer in Gloucester Harbor.

In 1845 a German fossil hunter named Albert Koch announced that *he* had finally found the bones of an enormous and true sea serpent. He exhibited his monster in the Apollo saloon in New York City. Koch was exposed as a fraud but the bones he exhibited turned out to be real. They were the bones of the extinct whale, Zeuglodon, a 60-foot (18.2 meter) sea creature that lived more than 30 million years ago.

Zeuglodon looks a lot like the description of Hans Egede's monster. Is it possible that Zeuglodon was still alive in the deep seas only two hundred years ago?

Koch had put the bones of two Zeuglodons together to make his fossil more impressive, added a few extras to dress it up, and built some humps into the skeleton.

*Koch's "sea monster" on exhibit in New York City.*

*Zeuglodon might have looked like this.*

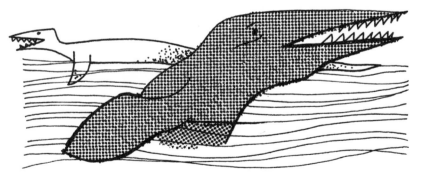

Koch's hoax made scientists warier than ever of associating themselves with sea monsters.

As the argument raged on, scientists pointed out that the people who reported sea serpents were not trained observers and that they really didn't know what they were looking at when they saw unusual things in the ocean.

In 1848 Captain Peter M'Quhae of Her Majesty's Ship *Daedalus* reported that he and his officers had watched a sea serpent in the Atlantic Ocean, near the Cape of Good Hope. Their description of its length, size, speed, and appearance was careful and specific. Captain M'Quhae, in his report to the Admiralty, said that the serpent passed so close to the ship that "had it been a man of my acquaintance, I should easily have recognized his features with my naked eye."

*The* Daedalus *sea serpent.*

*Sir Richard Owen*

The account brought on an argument between M'Quhae and Sir Richard Owen, a noted scientist. Richard Owen was a famous and respected authority on the anatomy of vertebrates—animals with backbones—both living and extinct. He was the man who gave dinosaurs their name. Owen said that the animal Captain M'Quhae and his officers described was a giant seal.

There were many more sea-serpent sightings but respectable seafaring men were so ridiculed for their descriptions of monsters that they stopped reporting them.

In 1893, some years after the *Daedalus* sighting, another sea captain, Captain Cringle, observed a sea monster from aboard his ship, *Umfuli*. It was a calm, sunny day and they were near the Cape of Good Hope. The captain, his mate, and the crew watched for half an hour through field glasses. Later that day the mate described the sea serpent in the ship's log. He said that its shape was like a conger eel, but about 80 feet (24.3 meters) long.

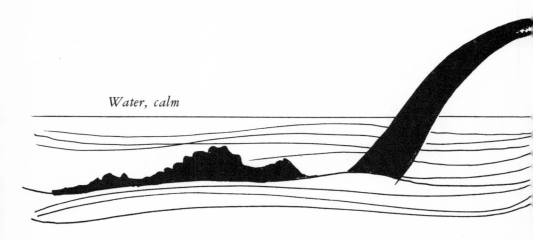

Water, calm

*Captain Cringle and his mate reported that the sea serpent they saw was about 80 feet long, with a head like a conger eel.*

Although the report was recorded in the ship's log, Captain Cringle was so worried about being laughed at that he didn't talk about the sighting for thirty-five years.

Sir Richard Owen continued to be unconvinced that sea serpents existed. He kept asking: Why don't scientists see them?

Some did. In 1905 two British naturalists, Fellows of the Royal Zoological Society, were on a scientific cruise aboard the yacht *Valhalla* when they saw a large animal in the sea, off the coast of Brazil. They reported that it

*Water, calm*

*Meade-Waldo and Nicoll, the scientists on the* Valhalla, *said that their sea serpent was dark brown above and whitish below.*

had " . . . a large fin or frill, about 6 feet long . . . a great head and neck of the same thickness . . . and dark brown above, whitish below. . . . The head and the eye had a turtle-like appearance."

The naturalists agreed that it must be the animal called the great sea serpent but they didn't agree on what kind of animal it was. One thought that it seemed to be a reptile because of the shape of the head and the eye. The other thought it was more likely to be some sort of mammal since its mouth did not extend back past the eye as a reptile's mouth does.

Anton Cornelius Oudemans, a Dutch biologist, wrote a biography of sea serpents that was published in 1892. After examining and analyzing many reports, he concluded that the sea serpent was no reptile, but a mammal—a giant, long-necked seal. But Oudemans pictures this unknown kind of seal as being shaped almost exactly like an extinct reptile, the plesiosaur, which lived at the time of the dinosaurs.

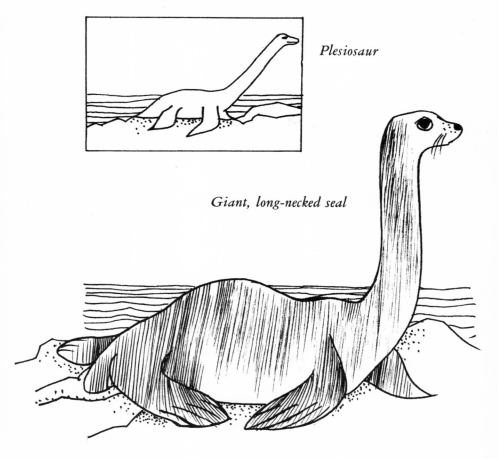

*Plesiosaur*

*Giant, long-necked seal*

In 1968 a Belgian scientist, Dr. Bernard Heuvelmans, published a book called *In the Wake of the Sea Serpents*. Dr. Heuvelmans classified almost 600 sea-serpent sightings from 1639 to 1966. He divided the believable ones (those which were seen by trained and careful observers) into groups:

MAMMALS

1. A long-necked, tailless mammal.

2. The Merhorse—a mammal with a tail, a mane, and a horselike head.

3. A very long, many-humped mammal with a short head and neck and one pair of flippers.

4.   A long mammal with rows of triangular "fins."

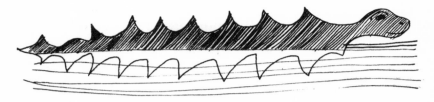

5.   A mammal that looked like a giant otter.

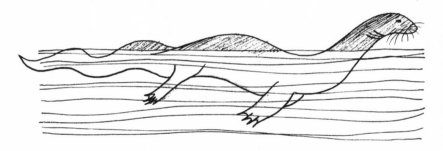

REPTILES
   1.   A reptile that looked like an enormous crocodile.

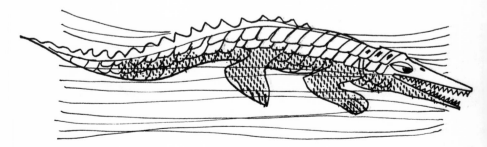

2.    Some kind of giant turtle.

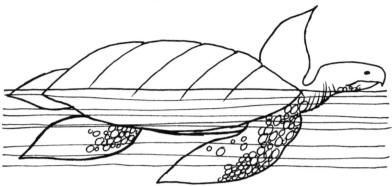

AN AMPHIBIAN—some kind of giant tadpole.

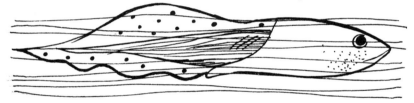

A FISH—something like a huge eel.

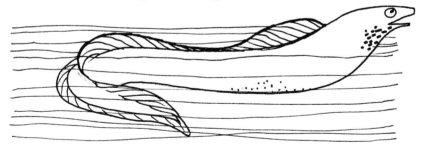

Are these descriptions of sea monsters anything like the descriptions of the Monster in Loch Ness?

What does that monster look like? Who has seen it? What did they say?

WORLD INTEREST
ROUSED
MONSTER INQ' 7

round Loch Ness, in
verness-shire, people
the week-end were
g the long stretch of
n the hope of getting a
iew of the "monster"
d to be living in its
ious depth

been repor
en seen of
s recently
Loch Ness r
orld-wide int
and commer
wspapers of
in museun
ggestions abo
ises, while sailors and trav-
e to give evidence that th
es have seen just such
elsewhere.

£20,000
FOR THE
MONSTER.

Daily
and M

No. 27,165.                WEDNESDAY,

LOCH NESS MONSTE

WHAT IS IT ?              100 PEOP

Sworn Statement
By
Foyers Photographer GREA

RE THERE
WO IN THE
LOCH?

30-ft. Beast seen
for an Hour

3

## We Have Seen the Monster!

O VER THE YEARS the people who lived
around Loch Ness talked among themselves about the
creature in the loch, but they didn't talk about it to
strangers. Maybe, because they were afraid of being
laughed at. Maybe, because they thought it was an evil
omen to see it. Some people said that the devil itself
lived in Loch Ness.

46

But when the new road was built in 1933 there was a lot more coming and going around the lake. People began to report seeing the Monster. People began talking about it.

On April 14, 1933, Mr. and Mrs. John Mackay were driving home from Inverness along the new road. It was a calm, bright sunny afternoon. Mr. Mackay was driving. Mrs. Mackay looked over at the loch.

"I saw a violent commotion in the water, then two large black humps moving in a line. The back hump was bigger than the front one. They rose and sank in an undulating manner. Together they stretched for about 20 feet [about 6 meters]."

Mrs. Mackay grabbed her husband, who slammed on the brakes. Together they watched "an enormous animal" until it turned and plunged under the water, making a huge wave that rolled into the shore.

The Mackays owned the inn at Drumnadrochit and they were afraid that people would think that their story was a publicity story to get business for the inn.

But they told the story to their friend Alex Campbell. Alex Campbell was the water bailie on Loch Ness—the warden in charge of protecting the salmon fishing there. He lived right on the shore. He knew fish and he knew the loch.

Alex Campbell was also a reporter for the local newspaper, the *Inverness Courier*, and he wrote up the story for the paper. It was published on May 2, 1933. Alex Campbell thought that it was about time to start reporting the sightings. He said that he had seen the creature himself several times over the years. He saw it again a few days later.

"It had a long, tapering neck, about 6 feet long, and a smallish head with a serpentine look about it, and a huge hump behind which I reckoned was about 30 feet long. It was turning its head constantly."

The editor of the *Inverness Courier* said that if the animal was as big as Alex Campbell and the Mackays said, then it was a real monster. And that's how the

*Alex Campbell*

creature in Loch Ness got its name. It has a pet name, too. People call it Nessie.

On July 22, 1933, there was another kind of sighting. The Monster was ashore!

"It was crossing the road. It was fairly big, with a high back, and it seemed to have a long neck which moved up and down in the manner of a scenic railway. It was a terrible, dark elephant gray, of a loathsome texture, reminiscent of a snail."

That was the way Mr. and Mrs. George Spicer described their meeting with the Monster.

The Monster was even more of a shock to them because neither of them had ever even heard of it! They were driving slowly along General Wade's Road. It was about four o'clock in the afternoon. Suddenly, about 200 yards (180 meters) ahead of them, they saw a huge animal crossing the road. It was partly across when they saw it, coming out of the underbrush on one side and disappearing into the ferns and bushes on the other. Because the Monster was slightly below a rise in the road at that place, this is about what they saw:

They couldn't see the head or legs or a tail if there was one. The Spicers weren't sure of the animal's size but the road at that place is 12 feet (3.6 meters) wide, and the part they saw stretched across it.

Mr. Spicer sped up to the spot and jumped out of the car. He could see where the animal had crushed down the ferns, but it had disappeared into the loch.

During 1933 the Monster was seen several times on land. It was seen on the beach, in the ferns, and making its way up the mouths of the rivers flowing into Urquhart Bay.

On Sunday, November 12, 1933, Mr. Hugh Gray, a farmer who lived next to the loch, was taking a walk. He was near where the Foyers River comes into Loch Ness and he was carrying his camera. Mr. Gray saw a lot of splashing in the loch and took the first known photograph of the Monster.

*Hugh Gray's photograph.*

He said that it was "an object of considerable dimensions, rising two or three feet above the water, dark gray in color with a smooth and glistening skin. It made a great disturbance, throwing up a lot of spray."

Mr. Gray took five pictures. Only one came out.

A scientist from the British Museum of Natural History examined the picture. He said that it was not a living thing, but a rotting tree trunk which natural gases had caused to rise suddenly to the surface of the loch.

On Friday, January 5, 1934, Mr. Arthur Grant, a young veterinary student, was riding home on his motorcycle just after midnight when a large animal "bounded" across the road in front of him. It was a bright, moonlit night.

"I had a splendid view of the object," he said. "In fact I almost struck it with my motorcycle."

He said that it had a long neck, large oval eyes at the top of a small head, a huge body, and a large, roundish tail. He saw flippers in the front and he thought—but he wasn't sure—flippers in back. He thought it was 15 or 20 feet (about 5 or 6 meters) long.

Arthur Grant got off his motorcycle and chased the animal but it splashed into the loch and disappeared. As soon as he got home he made a quick drawing of what he had seen.

Arthur Grant knew a lot about animals but he said he had never seen an animal like that one—it looked like a cross between some kind of seal and a plesiosaur.

Some students at Edinburgh College and their teacher, who was a Fellow of the Zoological Society of Scotland, happened to be staying in the neighborhood.

*Arthur Grant's drawing looked something like this.*

They spent the next couple of days looking for signs of the animal on the bank where it had disappeared. They found soft tracks that might have been made by flippers or sliding feet. And they found a place up the beach, in the ferns, that was all smashed down as if a big animal had been lying there. There were flipper prints nearby.

They measured all the prints and the distance from print to print. When they got back to college they compared the prints with those of known animals and finally said that the prints were the kind that might have been made by a walrus.

In April 1934, Dr. Kenneth Wilson, a London surgeon, was on vacation in Scotland. He was standing on a cliff looking down at the loch when he saw a disturbance in the water. He ran back to the car, grabbed his camera, and took two pictures.

In all the years since, there has never been a clearer picture of the Monster than Dr. Wilson's first picture. It caused great excitement when it was printed in the newspapers. Because Dr. Wilson did not want any publicity, his name was not used, and the picture was called "The Surgeon's Photograph." (It is still known by that name.)

*The Surgeon's Photograph.*

*Associated Newspapers*

Again, there was a lot of argument among scientists. One said that it was simply a floating log.

Another said that it was the tail of an otter, diving.

Still another said that it was the dorsal fin of a killer whale, though he did not explain how the whale got through the locks in the canal and into Loch Ness without being seen.

Since 1934, thousands of people have reported seeing the Monster.

Most of them have seen it in the water.

What most people see is humps—one, two, three— even more. And they report humps of different sizes, or say that the humps change size.

## WHAT PEOPLE HAVE REPORTED SEEING IN LOCH NESS

*Humps—one or many*

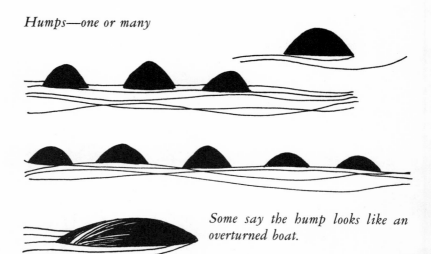

*Some say the hump looks like an overturned boat.*

Some people report seeing a long neck and a tiny head—like a snake or a turtle or an eel or a horse. Some people say that they didn't see any eyes. Some report eyes like a snake's, or large oval eyes, like a seal's.

Some people say the animal has small horns. Some say there is a mane on the long neck. They report different kinds of skin—smooth, slimy, rough, scaly, furry.

Most people say that the Monster is dark—gray or black or brown. Some, who have gotten a better look, say that it is dark above and light-colored underneath. (That's the way most sea serpents are described, too.)

Almost everyone says that it is very big and very fast; that it makes a V-shaped wake in the water and that it doesn't like noise.

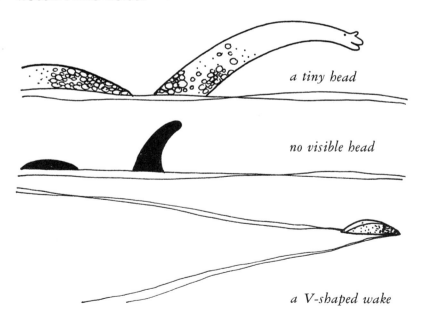

*a tiny head*

*no visible head*

*a V-shaped wake*

Quite a few people have reported seeing the Monster ashore. Some have made careful drawings of what they saw. Some of the drawings look like this:

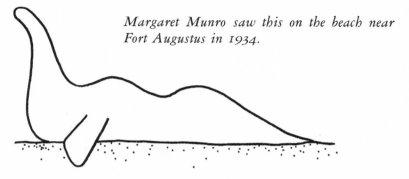

*Margaret Munro saw this on the beach near Fort Augustus in 1934.*

*Torquil MacCleod reported watching this animal through binoculars for 9 minutes, in 1960. The binocular markings showed the size—40–50 feet, he thought.*

Most people who saw it ashore said that the Monster had flippers. Some said that it had short, thick legs and that it moved on the front legs and dragged the back ones.

A few people said that the Monster looked like an elephant or a hippopotamus or even a camel. But most of them said that it looked like a dinosaur or an unusual kind of seal.

Can the Monster change size and shape?

Are there big animals and little ones?

Have people been seeing different kinds of animals?

The Monster in Loch Ness is one of the biggest mysteries around. And the first big question is: Is the Monster real?

Most scientists say no. Here's why.

Up to now, there is no real proof that the Monster exists. If there are huge animals living in Loch Ness, why is it that no one has ever found a body, a skeleton,

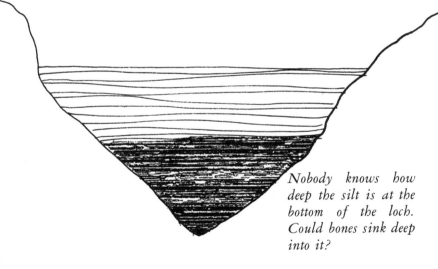

*Nobody knows how deep the silt is at the bottom of the loch. Could bones sink deep into it?*

or even a single unexplained bone? Why isn't there a really clear photograph that scientists can study?

But—in the last fifty years or so, almost four thousand people say that they have seen it. They have seen it up close and far away. They have described what they saw in great detail. Sometimes groups of people have watched it together, from cars and buses, standing on the road or on a pier, or from boats on the loch.

Is the weight of so many reports some kind of proof?

There's a lot to think about:

How reliable are eyewitness accounts? Do people always know what they are seeing?

Do most people accept as fact only the things they *know* exist?

What is the value of knowing what the thing in the loch is?

Does it even matter if the Monster is real?

Who cares?

*Torquil MacCleod, one of the first full-time monster hunters.*

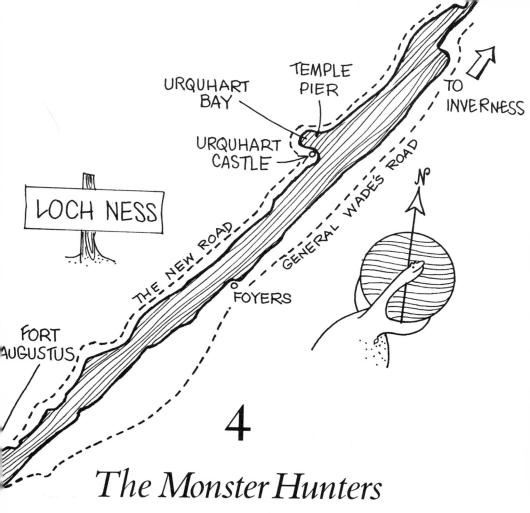

# 4

# *The Monster Hunters*

Even though many people don't take the idea of a monster in Loch Ness seriously, a lot of people do. Some are dedicated and curious enough to become full-time monster hunters. Others spend a little while—maybe a few weeks a year, or even a few days—trying to put the facts together, or to get some sort of proof that the Monster exists.

## Summer 1933

The first serious investigator was Lt. Commander R. T. Gould of the Royal Navy. Three years before, Commander Gould had published a book called *The Case for the Sea Serpent*, which was made up of many accounts, by experienced seamen, of sea-serpent sightings. He checked the accounts in ships' logs and naval records. Commander Gould had concluded that people had been seeing several different kinds of sea monsters: an unknown kind of long-necked seal; some kind of giant turtle; some animal like a prehistoric plesiosaur.

Armed with a camera and binoculars, Commander Gould circled Loch Ness twice on his motorcycle, *Cynthia.* He talked with about fifty eyewitnesses, again checking stories carefully.

### *Commander Gould's Conclusions*

Most of the witnesses were serious and truthful people who believed they had actually seen a large, unknown animal.

The habits of sea serpents and those of the Loch Ness Monster were so similar that the Monster *must* be a great sea serpent that had somehow gotten into the loch.

Comparing the statements of all the eyewitnesses he interviewed that summer, he came up with a description of the animal:

It was 45 feet (about 13.5 meters) long, of which the

head and neck were 10 feet (about 3 meters), the body 20 feet (about 6.5 meters), and the tail 15 feet (about 4.5 meters). It was humped, with a small, flat head on a long neck. Its color was dark brown and got lighter as it dried. Its skin was rough with a dark ridge on the back, and it had at least two flippers.

*45 feet (about 13.5 meters)*

| *15 feet* | *20 feet* | *10 feet* |
| *(about 4.5 meters)* | *(about 6 meters)* | *(about 3 meters)* |

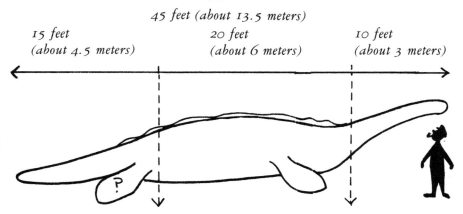

*Commander Gould's idea of the Monster.*

But he had a new idea about the kind of animal it might be—not a reptile or a mammal but an amphibian, some sort of giant newt. (Some boat and dock men who worked around the loch used to call Nessie "the salamander.")

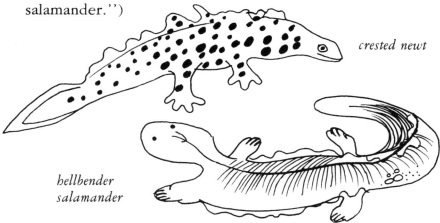

*crested newt*

*hellbender salamander*

## 1933 and 1936

Movies were another tool investigators used. In 1933 and 1936 Malcom Irvine, a Scotch filmmaker, along with a newsreel crew took several films that were supposed to show the Monster swimming by. But the films were unclear and of poor quality, and many people are unsure whether the films are real or a hoax. The originals have disappeared.

## July 1934

The next serious investigator was Sir Edward Mountain, chairman of a large insurance company. He was spending the summer in a castle on the loch. Sir Edward hired a team of twenty unemployed men from Inverness. He gave each one a camera and a pair of field glasses, and every morning for five weeks he brought them out to the loch by bus, where they watched all day.

The monster watchers had a number of sightings and took some unclear photographs and films. One detailed sighting added an interesting fact. The watcher described the animal's head as having stumpy horns.

Sir Edward presented the film and the reports to some London zoologists, who decided that the animal was a gray seal. Sir Edward said afterward that the zoologists should simply have said that they didn't know what the animal was.

## 1935

Dr. Constance Whyte went to live near the loch when her husband, an engineer, became manager of the Caledonian Canal. She became interested in the Monster because so many eyewitnesses seemed to be such sensible and intelligent people. But until she began interviewing people who had seen it, she did not believe in the Monster herself.

Between 1935 and 1955 she spoke at length with about a hundred eyewitnesses and evaluated their accounts. These are detailed in her book, *More Than A Legend* which was published in 1957.

*Dr. Constance Whyte.*

### Dr. Whyte's Conclusions

There was not one unknown animal in Loch Ness but a colony of animals that had lived there over a long period of time, reproducing and raising families.

The animals were not peculiar to Loch Ness. There were legends of similar animals in many deep Scottish lakes.

Dr. Whyte had no opinion as to what kind of animals the creatures were.

## July 14, 1951

Investigators have always tried to get a good, clear photograph, but since the Surgeon's Photograph there have been very few that were either clear or helpful.

On July 14, 1951, Lachlan Stuart, a woodcutter who lived near the loch, got this picture from about 50 yards (45 meters) away.

*Lachlan Stuart's photograph.*

When Mr. Stuart snapped the picture only the humps were in the frame, but he and a friend who was with him also described the animal's head. They said it was about the size and shape of a sheep's head, on a long neck.

The animal kept bobbing its head up and down in the water and they thought it was chasing fish. They agreed that the biggest hump was about 3 feet (.9 meters) out of the water.

*Conclusions*

If the humps could be photographed, they were real. The humps were different sizes.

## 1955

Photographs continued to be the only evidence. One photograph that helped to establish the size of the Monster was taken by Mr. P. A. Macnab.

Urquhart Castle is 64 feet (19.5 meters) high. If you compare the size of the two humps with the ruins of the castle, you can see how big the animal seems to be.

66

*P. A. Macnab's photograph.*

Copyright, P. A. Macnab

## Conclusions

The large hump is about 50 feet (15.2 meters) long.
This might be two animals, a large one and a small
one.

Of course some of the investigators have wound up
being nonbelievers. The zoologist Dr. Maurice Burton
started as a believer. After thirty years of investigating
he changed his mind.

## Dr. Burton's Conclusions

The Monster might be many kinds of things, all of
them perfectly normal. It might be mats of decaying
vegetation, giving off gases that make them move. It
might be deer and otters swimming in the loch. It might
be birds or boats.

*Tim Dinsdale on watch at Loch Ness.*        *Courtesy of Tim Dinsdale*

## April 1960

Tim Dinsdale, an aeronautical engineer, began his investigation. He has since become a full-time monster hunter.

Dinsdale had a movie camera with a telephoto lens. On his sixth day of investigating, he took about a minute and a half of film of a moving object in the loch. The film shows a dark, hump-shaped object zigzagging across the loch until it disappears.

The thing in the water left a V-shaped wake—the same kind that witnesses had been reporting for years.

Within an hour, Dinsdale made another film to compare with the first one. The second film showed a moving motorboat in about the same place the Monster had been.

You can see that the wakes look different.

*Monster wake*

*Motorboat wake*

Over the years, Dinsdale has made a number of different kinds of investigations, both on his own and with fellow monster hunters.

### Dinsdale's Conclusions

The Monster is some kind of plesiosaur.

Although plesiosaurs were air breathers, the Monster does not have to come up to breathe often because the humps are air sacs in which it stores the air it gets on the surface. Then it uses that air up slowly, under the water.

*During the Mesozoic Era, about 200 million years ago, there were several kinds of plesiosaurs.*

*Courtesy of Tim Dinsdale*

*Loch Ness Phenomena Investigation Bureau camera watch at Urquhart Bay.*

## 1961—1962

Constance Whyte, along with naturalists Peter Scott and Richard Fitter, Member of Parliament David James, and Norman Collins from ATV (a television company in England) got together to organize the Loch Ness Phenomena Investigation Bureau. In time they were joined by other members. Their aim was to collect eyewitness accounts and to try to get photographs.

By 1967 they were maintaining a full volunteer camera watch over 70 percent of the loch from May through October.

They analyzed reported sightings carefully and accepted those which seemed to be authentic.

# LOCH NESS PHENOMENA INVESTIGATION BUREAU LTD ( By Guarantee )

25 Ashley Place, London S.W.1

## SIGHTING REPORT

Name of Witness ...............................................

of (*address*) ......................................

..........................................

........................................

Occupation .................................................Age ..........................................

Witness' Position near Loch ...................................................... Date .......................

Estimated distance of object from witness .....................................

    ,,     direction of object from witness — (a) By reference to landmarks ..........................................

                        (b) By Bearing (true) expressed in 360 degree notation change of arc ..............................................

    ,,     speed of object ....................................................

            Grounds for estimated speed ........................................

    ,,    time length of episode in minutes .............. Time of commencement .......................

                                   Time of conclusion ........................................

Direction of object travelling (a) Landmarks .................

                           (b) Compass ...................

Colour ...........................................................

Texture ...............................................

**ESTIMATED OVER ALL LENGTH OF OBJECT**

Was one object observed or more than one ...................... ......................................................

If more than one were they moving together or separately .........................................................

Height out of water of each object .........................................................................................

Were there any craft in the vicinity .............. If so where .......................................................

Was there a wash .........................................................................................................................

Any other associated phenomenon ..........................................................................................

Was the object seen to surface .................................................................................................

Was the object seen to submerge ..............................................................................................

Did the object react to sound, e.g. boat, road vehicle, aircraft ..............................................

Do you believe the object was alive .........................................................................................

Photographed by ........................................................................................................................

Camera used ...............................................................................................................................

Film type ......................................................................................................................................

Film footage ................................. Take 1 ....................... Take 2 .......................

Take 3 ....................... Take 4 ................ ...... ...

Aperture setting ..........................................................................................................................

Meter reading .............................. ............................................................................................

Filter ...........................................................................................................................................

Weather conditions ....................................................................................................................

Direction of wind .......................................................................................................................

Condition of surface of water .................................................................................................

Visibility   (a) Type ........................... (b) Furthest object visible to witness
in direction of observation ...............................................

Type and magnification of binoculars ......................................................................................

May your name be published in any report, article or book? ....................................................

They added to the list of things which seemed characteristic of the Monster.

It sank straight down when submerging.

It almost always appeared on calm, windless days.

From the last conclusion, F. W. Holiday, a newspaper man and a member of the investigation, made a conclusion of his own:

The Monster is some kind of great worm.

Worms have soft, moist skins that dry out on windy days. He thought that even larger worms were the origin of all the sea-serpent stories.

Holiday believed that the Loch Ness Monster was a descendant of a prehistoric, wormlike creature called the Tulley monster. Fossils of the Tulley monster have been found, but the largest are only 14 inches (35 centimeters) long.

*Tulley monster*

After Constance Whyte retired, the Investigation Bureau was joined by Dr. Roy Mackal, a professor of biochemistry from the University of Chicago. He became the chief scientist.

### Dr. Mackal's conclusion:

The Monster was some kind of giant water slug. (Dr. Mackal, who has continued to investigate the mystery, has since changed his mind in favor of a giant, unknown kind of amphibian, or a kind of thick, monster eel.)

*Dr. Mackal's amphibian*

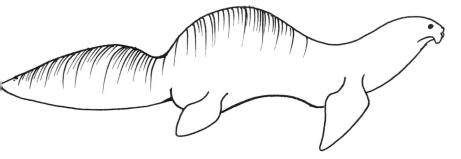

*Dr. Mackal's eel*

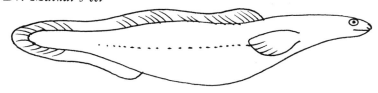

Gradually the Investigation Bureau got money grants from a number of places for additional experiments to help the investigation along. But with all the telescopes on still and motion-picture cameras, no indisputable pictures were taken.

# 1962

Colonel H. G. Hassler brought his junk-rigged boat, the *Jester*, into Loch Ness because he thought that a quiet sailboat would be better for observing the Monster than a noisy motorboat. (Monster hunters say that one reason sea serpents aren't observed anymore is because ships are too noisy.)

The crew of the *Jester* put down hydrophones to listen for underwater sounds. They heard clicking noises at the same time they observed humps in the water.

Only mammals such as dolphins and whales make underwater sounds to help them find prey and to communicate with each other.

The same year, an expedition from Oxford and Cambridge universities explored the loch with an echo sounder. They recorded echoes of large, moving objects in places where there had been a number of sightings.

## HOW SOUND WORKS TO "HEAR" UNDERWATER OBJECTS

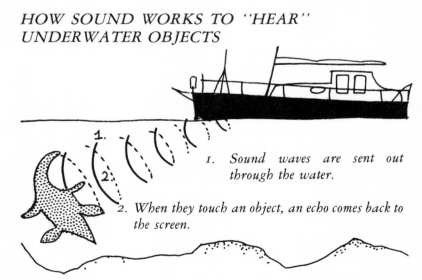

1.  Sound waves are sent out through the water.

2. When they touch an object, an echo comes back to the screen.

*Sonar uses sound to detect underwater objects, still and moving.*

The expedition also took samples of the stuff at the bottom of the loch and found a thick layer of dead, organic material—plants, animals, and plankton. Some water animals—including some very big ones—feed on this.

## 1963

The Loch Ness Phenomena Investigation Bureau tried blasting some of the rocks around the lake to try to re-create the 1933 conditions when the road was being built and the modern sightings began.

There were forty sightings in that summer of 1963.

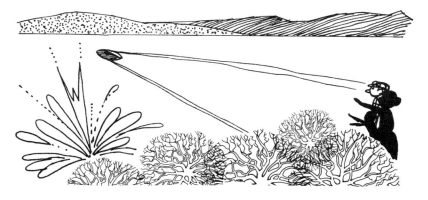

## 1965

David James got the Joint Air Reconnaissance Intelligence Center of the RAF to use their special equipment to interpret the Dinsdale film.

They reported that the shape was "probably an animate object, that it might be anywhere from 30 to 92 feet long, about 6 feet wide, and 5 feet high and moving at a considerable speed."

Many experts disagreed. They said that the report was only an opinion and that the quality of the film was so poor that the opinion could be wrong.

## 1967–1968

The University of Birmingham, England, set up sonar equipment that picked up underwater echoes. These echoes were analyzed as coming from animate (living) objects.

Other scientists said that although the objects on the recording were moving, they might be masses of peat giving off gases that made them move up and down.

## 1969

A small yellow submarine, the *Viperfish*, went down into the loch and didn't see a thing. Dan Taylor, the young American oceanographer who operated the sub said that down in the loch the farthest he could see in any direction was 12 inches (30 centimeters).

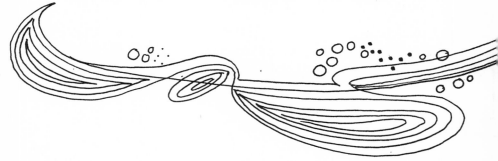

But he had some scary experiences. Once the pressure hatch was jolted partly open. Another time the whole submarine was picked up and whirled around by unknown forces.

The *Viperfish* also carried dart guns attached to the sub, which could be activated from inside. Their purpose was to get a specimen of the Monster's skin to be analyzed.

At about the same time another sub, the Vickers'
*Pisces*, was helping to make a Sherlock Holmes film
about the Monster in the Loch. The *Pisces* was pulling a
fake monster, which broke away and sank. They never
found their monster but they did locate an unexpected
trench, over 900 feet (274 meters) deep, in the bottom
of the loch.

*National Film Archive, London*

Could some later pictures and sonar contacts be of the lost movie monster?

## 1970

A team from the Academy of Applied Sciences of Boston, Massachusetts, headed by Dr. Robert Rines, tackled the mystery with a variety of new approaches and new scientific tools. They concentrated on Urquhart Bay, where the Monster is most often seen.

They tried scientifically prepared Monster love potions—smells they thought might attract it. They tried to tempt its appetite with tasty lures. No success.

They tried towing a side-scan sonar device back and forth under the surface of the loch in Urquhart Bay. They tried anchoring the side-scan sonar to Temple Pier.

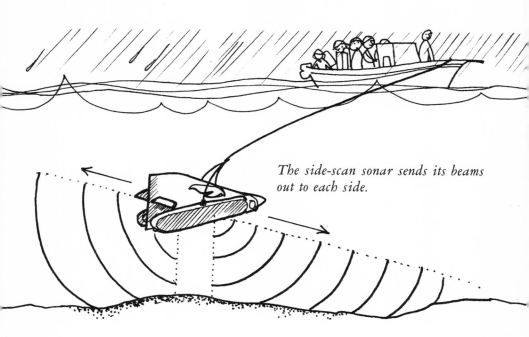

*The side-scan sonar sends its beams out to each side.*

On September 21, the side-scanner on the pier detected two large objects passing through its beam. Soon after, one of the objects passed back, going the other way.

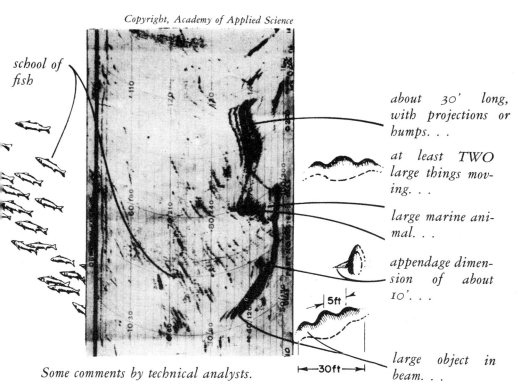

school of fish

about 30' long, with projections or humps. . .

at least TWO large things moving. . .

large marine animal. . .

appendage dimension of about 10'. . .

large object in beam. . .

5ft

*Some comments by technical analysts.*

30ft

The side-scan sonar also revealed what might be caves in the steep sides of the loch—a possible habitat for large underwater creatures. Could there be air spaces in the caves?

The survey also showed that there were deep channels in the bottom of the loch.

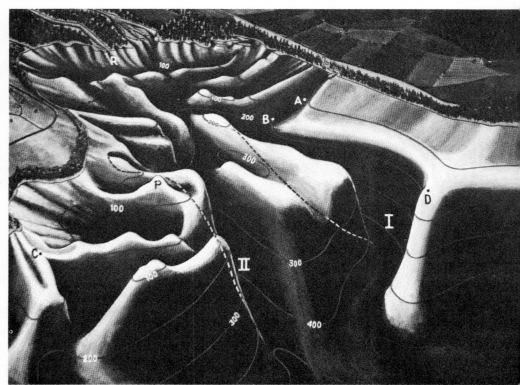

*Underwater chart of Urquhart Bay.*

## 1971 and 1972

The Academy team concentrated on trying to get a close-up picture of a monster. They used underwater stroboscopic lights, synchronized with automatic cameras that took a picture every 15 seconds.

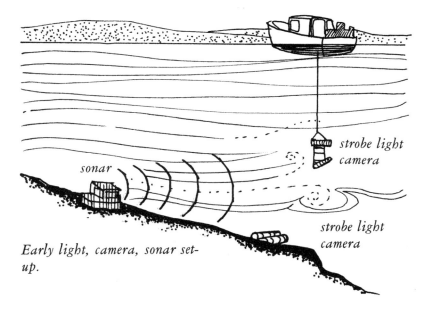

*sonar*

*strobe light camera*

*strobe light camera*

*Early light, camera, sonar set-up.*

The team spent many days and nights patrolling likely parts of the loch—places where there had been the most sightings.

Sometimes the equipment was anchored on the bottom. Sometimes it was suspended from one of the boats.

The area covered by the camera lens was also monitored by sonar beams.

## 1971

Nothing.

## August 7, 1972

Sonar picked up the trace of a large, moving object. The cameras got a picture.

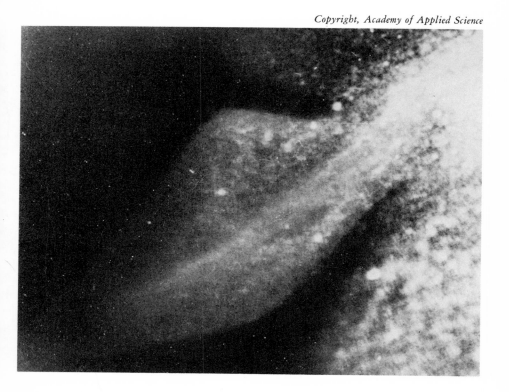

Four frames of the film shot that night showed what appeared to be some kind of flipper attached to a creature's body. Photo technicians estimated the size of the flipper to be from 6 to 8 feet (1.8 to 2.4 meters) long by 2 to 4 feet (.6 to 1.2 meters) wide.

The picture was sent to the Jet Propulsion Laboratory at Cal Tech and made sharper by a special computer scanning process. (The same process is used to define the NASA pictures that space-probe cameras take of the planets.)

Scientists around the world were impressed with the photographs but could not agree about the animal that was attached to the flipper. Some scientists said that the flipper looked a lot like the paddle of a plesiosaur.

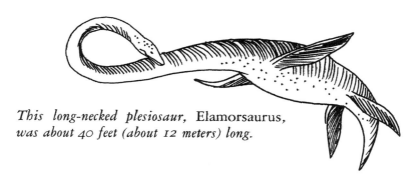

*This long-necked plesiosaur,* Elamorsaurus, *was about 40 feet (about 12 meters) long.*

## 1973

The Academy team tried again, with more sophisticated sonar-triggered underwater cameras. No success.

## June 20, 1975

They got these pictures, which were also put through the computer-scanner.

Is this the head of the Monster?

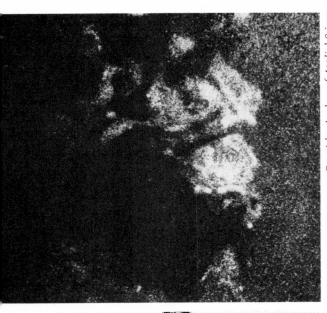

*Some scientists say that the photograph shows four "horns."*

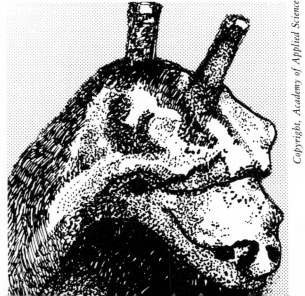

*The drawn interpretation of the head photo shows two horns.*

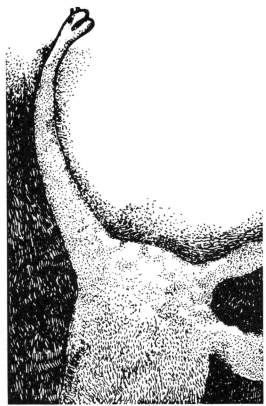

*Photograph of whole animal?*

*Drawn interpretation of the whole animal photograph.*

Is this the Monster from underneath?

Once again, scientists argued that as "evidence" the pictures were open to many interpretations. The Monster was still a mystery. But the investigators kept working.

## Summer, 1976

The Academy team was back in Loch Ness with more sophisticated tools—underwater television cameras and monitors, more sensitive sonar and camera equipment. But there was an even more important difference in this summer's experiments. A number of respected scientists—biologists, zoologists, paleontologists—no longer regarded the Loch Ness Monster as a joke. They were taking the accumulated bits of evidence seriously. They felt that the mystery was worth continuing investigation.

The Monster was changing from a legend into a real animal.

# 5

# *Will the Real Monster Please Rise?*

IN 1938 A COELACANTH (see-la-canth), a five-foot-long prehistoric fish that was supposed to be extinct for 70 million years, was fished out of the Indian Ocean, off the African coast. Since then a number have been caught, always in the same location, the deep and narrow Mozambique Channel.

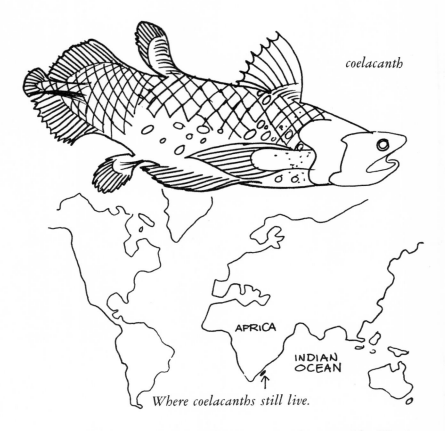

coelacanth

APRICA

INDIAN
OCEAN

*Where coelacanths still live.*

Once coelacanths lived all over the world. Their fossils have been found everywhere. But their fossil record stopped along with those of the dinosaurs and the plesiosaurs. Somehow a group of coelacanths kept living and reproducing in the Mozambique Channel, because they were well adapted to that one small environment. It gave them everything the species needed to survive.

Whatever the creature in Loch Ness is, if it is any living animal, it must abide by the rules that govern life all over earth. No one has ever found any kind of animal, from the biggest whale to the most microscopic, one-celled creature, that was an exception to those rules.

It can't be a totally new kind of animal. It must be either the descendant of some kind of animal that once lived on earth or an animal that has been here all along. But it might be a *mutation*—a familiar animal that has become changed in important ways.

*Every animal on earth is a descendant of earlier animals:*

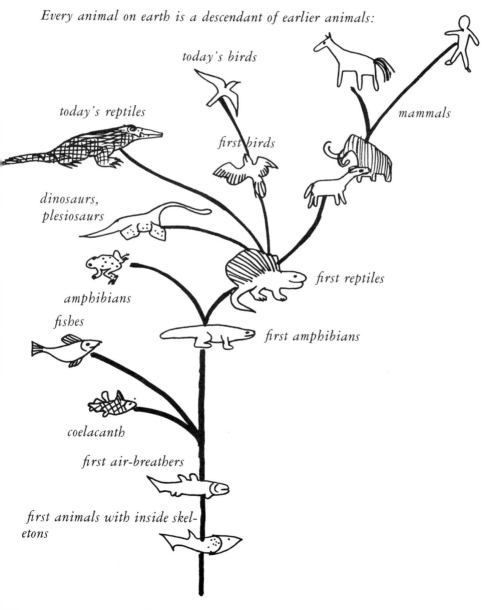

today's birds

today's reptiles

mammals

first birds

dinosaurs, plesiosaurs

first reptiles

amphibians

first amphibians

fishes

coelacanth

first air-breathers

first animals with inside skeletons

It can't be an extinct animal that has come back. Once a kind of animal is extinct, that's the end of it. If there are any of that animal alive, it is not extinct.

The animal's environment—the particular place it lives in—must provide it with everything it needs to stay alive.

The animal must be adapted to that environment—suited to live in it and get what it needs from it.

If the environment changes, animals that are not adapted to live in the changed environment cannot survive. But when the environment changes, some groups of animals are better adapted than others to the new conditions. Those animals keep going, and the others die out. That's the way life survives, all over earth.

For a species—a particular kind of animal—to survive, it must be able to make new individuals like itself. If no new individuals are made, the species would die out, because no animals live forever. All animals die.

*For about 100 million years, dinosaurs, plesiosaurs and animals like them were perfectly adapted to their environment. They were the most important animals on Earth.*

These are all science concepts that we accept as facts. They are the rules we accept unless new facts are discovered to change or disprove them.

Ideas are not facts. But there are scientific ideas that we temporarily accept as facts because there is no proof that they are *not* true.

One of these is that dinosaurs, plesiosaurs, and animals like them have been extinct for 60 million years or more.

We get our information about animals that lived millions of years ago from their fossils. Fossils can be bones, shells, body prints, footprints, even impressions of shape or skin. Fossils are found in layers of earth stuff—usually rock—called *geological strata*. (Strata means layers.)

Since we have learned to figure out the earth time when each layer was formed, we can tell when the animals lived whose fossils are in that layer.

If the layer of the next time period shows no more fossils of the animal, we conclude that the animal was no longer around. It had become extinct.

But is *not* finding fossils *proof* that an animal did not live during a particular time period? Suppose some of them lived in an out-of-the-way place where no one has hunted for fossils? Suppose some lived in a place where fossils were not preserved?

In a way, a fossil is an accident. Something happened to a particular animal (or plant) to preserve a trace of it in some way. For every fossil animal that is found, there were thousands of animals like it that died without being preserved. In the 500 million years of life on earth, there are probably thousands of kinds of animals that lived without leaving any trace. We have no sure way of knowing that they lived at all, even though we can make guesses.

| YEARS AGO | FOSSILS FOUND |
|---|---|
| 10,000–60 million (Cenozoic Era) | Man, all kinds of mammals, modern fishes, insects, plants, trees.<br><br>No more dinosaurs or plesiosaurs. |
| 130 million–200 million (Mesozoic Era) | DINOSAURS! All kinds of reptiles, large and small; the first birds. Flowering plants; pine-like trees. |
| 230 million–500 million (Paleozoic Era) | Shelled animals; sea animals; fishes; the first amphibians; reptiles; insects.<br>The first land plants. |
| 750 million–1 billion (Proterozoic Era) | Simple plants; sponges; worms. |
| 2 billion (Archeozoic Era) | A few limey sea plants. |

Sometimes a living animal like a coelacanth turns up that was believed to be extinct because no fossil of it has been found later than a certain time.

The coelacanth isn't even the oldest ''living fossil.'' The tuatara, a lizard that has been found alive and well in New Zealand, has been around since before the dinosaurs. But no fossils of it have been found in strata later than 135 million years ago.

Dinosaurs lived during the Mesozoic Era, which began about 225 million years ago and ended about 60 million years ago. As far as anyone knows, after that the dinosaurs and their companion animals were extinct. There is no fossil record since then.

The dinosaurs and their other reptile companions were the most important animals on earth for about 100

*There were many successful kinds of reptiles:*

*flying reptiles*

*dinosaurs*

*fish-like reptiles*

*snake-necked reptiles*

*mammal-like reptiles*

million years. They were very successful animals, which means that they were adapted to whatever changes there were on earth over a very long time.

The dinosaurs themselves were land animals, though some of them spent most of their time in the shallow seas. Other kinds of reptiles were adapted to live in the water. The plesiosaurs were reptiles like that, though some kinds of plesiosaurs could move about on land as well, on their flippers.

Could Nessie be a reptile? Maybe a plesiosaur?

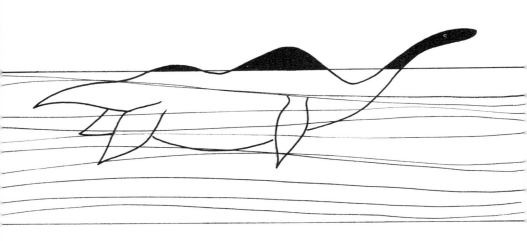

Some plesiosaurs looked almost exactly like many descriptions of Nessie. They had long necks and small heads, big bodies and long tails, and paddlelike flippers.

But would plesiosaurs still look like they did 70 million years ago? Or would they have evolved into a quite different-looking animal? Seventy million years ago the ancestors of people were about the size and shape of shrews.

Still, 70 million years ago oysters, mussels, turtles, and some other animals looked just about as they look today. Horseshoe crabs haven't changed for 200 million years. Their evolution stopped because they were well adapted to their environment.

*Plesiosaur fossil found in England.*

Once plesiosaurs did live in the area of Loch Ness. Their fossil bones have been found close by. Is it possible that a few groups of plesiosaurs still live in some deep lakes and maybe in the deep ocean?

Could a family of plesiosaurs live in the environment of Loch Ness?

Plesiosaurs lived in the salty seas, but they also lived in the estuaries of rivers—the places where rivers flow into the sea. The water there is a mixture of salt and fresh. Maybe, over a long time, plesiosaurs could adapt to fresh water. Remember, Loch Ness was cut off from the sea gradually, and the water changed from salt to fresh over a long, long period.

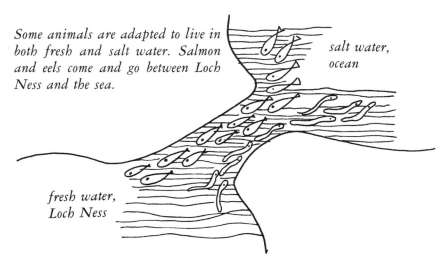

*Some animals are adapted to live in both fresh and salt water. Salmon and eels come and go between Loch Ness and the sea.*

salt water, ocean

fresh water, Loch Ness

Plesiosaurs were fish eaters and there are plenty of fish in the loch—enough to support a big family of plesiosaurs. A number of sighting accounts describe schools of fish swimming and jumping in panic before

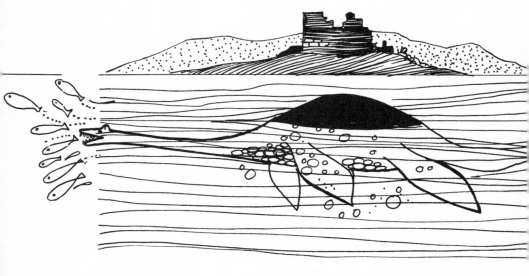

the fast-moving hump. Some accounts even describe Nessie fishing. And the Monster is often sighted at the mouths of rivers, where the salmon go up to spawn and young salmon come down into the loch.

But why don't people see the Monster even more, if it is a reptile? Like all reptiles, plesiosaurs were air breathers. They couldn't breathe underwater.

Plesiosaurs had their nostrils on top of their heads as today's crocodiles do. They could breathe with not much of themselves showing. And they may have evolved breathing tubes with the nostrils on top. Several eyewitnesses, from Sir Edward Mountain's team on, have described the Monster as having horns. When the Surgeon's Photo was computer-sharpened it seemed to show horns. So does the Rines' head picture.

All the dinosaurs were air breathers but some of those that lived in the water evolved different kinds of air storage chambers. They could store enough air to stay under water for a long time.

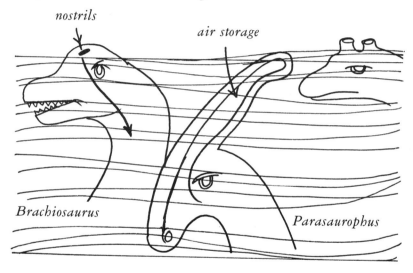

*nostrils*

*air storage*

*Brachiosaurus*

*Parasaurophus*

The temperature of the water in Loch Ness is a fact that argues against the Monster being a reptile. Reptiles are cold-blooded. That means that their temperature rises and falls to match the outside temperature around them. Snakes and turtles, lizards and crocodiles, don't live where it is very cold. Their heartbeat slows down so much that the blood almost stops flowing. Could a cold-blooded animal like a plesiosaur adapt to water as cold as that in Loch Ness?

As far as we know, there are no very large reptiles today, but scientists think that extremely large ones such as dinosaurs and plesiosaurs might have conserved their body heat better than the smaller reptiles that are around now. Some scientists even think they might have been warm-blooded.

Could Nessie be some other kind of reptile? Maybe a big snake, as the sea serpent was supposed to be?

Many people who have seen the Monster compare its head and eyes with those of a snake.

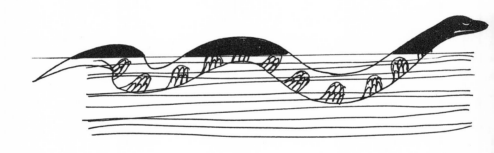

*Scientific drawing of the Great American Sea Serpent (after Heuvelmans).*

Or could the Monster be some kind of giant turtle? The majority of sightings are of only a big hump, "like the bottom of an overturned boat." Some people who have seen a head say it looks like a turtle's.

There are very big turtles but none nearly as big as the smallest monster is estimated to be. And no kind of giant turtle has ever lived in fresh water. Besides, a turtle's shell is hard and the humps seem to change size.

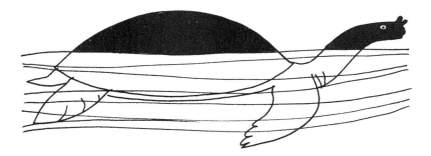

*Some species of turtles have very long necks. One kind has snorkel-like nostrils.*

Maybe the Monster isn't a reptile at all.
Could Nessie be some kind of mammal?
Some sightings have reported manes, whiskers, fur.
These are all hair and only mammals have hair.

Again, the problem with Nessie's being a mammal is
that mammals breathe air. They should be seen on the
surface more than Nessie is. Even mammals like whales
that live entirely in the water are often on top.
Could the Monster be a whale?

*head?*

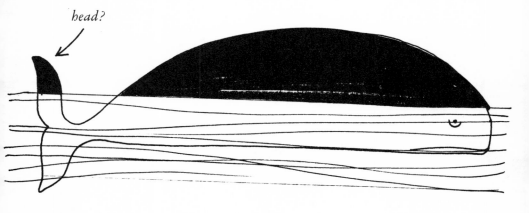

A whale is the only animal around today that seems to fit the size. And some witnesses describe "misty, blowing breath."

But huge sea mammals like whales are very visible on the surface. A family of whales could hardly stay out of sight in a lake.

What about a porpoise? Or a school of porpoises? Some people say that Nessie makes a noise like a porpoise blowing. Could three porpoises look like three humps?

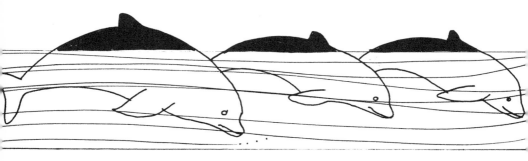

But porpoises are friendly and visible.
Could the Monster be a giant otter?

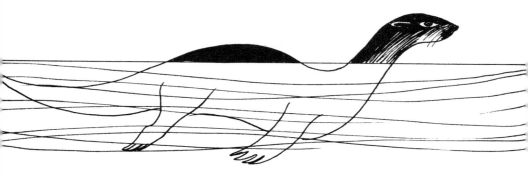

Some scientists who do agree that there is *something* in Loch Ness vote for an otter. There *are* otters in the loch. Some otters in the British Isles measure up to 7 feet (about 2 meters). That is very big for an otter, but not nearly as big as Nessie is supposed to be.

Some sea-serpent sightings have been described as looking like a kind of super-otter. But no one has actually ever seen a super-otter.

Could Nessie be a walrus? The zoologists who examined the tracks of Arthur Grant's animal said that they were exactly like walrus tracks. But walruses spend a lot of time on shore. And they certainly don't fit most of the descriptions of the Monster.

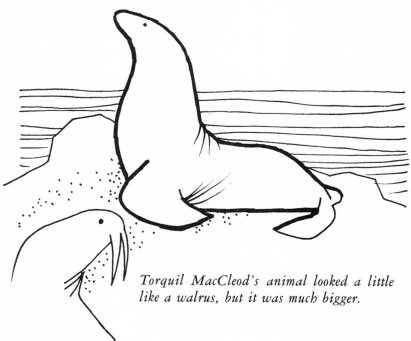

*Torquil MacCleod's animal looked a little like a walrus, but it was much bigger.*

Could Nessie be a seal?
Or several seals together?

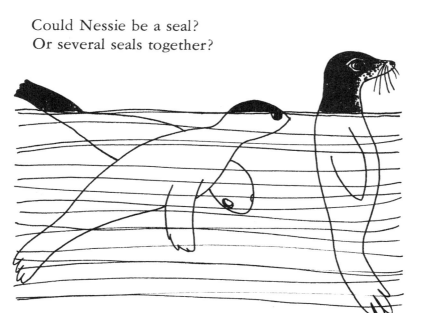

*Seals swimming under water take on a
shape like this.*

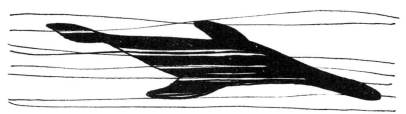

There certainly are a lot of seals on the coasts of
Scotland. There are so many that most of the people
there would recognize a seal, no matter where they saw
one. Besides, seals don't make waves when they swim.
They never swim with their heads under water and their
backs sticking up. They often get out of the water to
bask in the sun. They are friendly and curious, not shy.

Some scientists say that the Monster is a long-necked seal. Nobody has ever seen a long-necked seal, but possibly some may have evolved. All the water-living mammals we know have short necks or no necks.

Could the Monster be a sea cow?

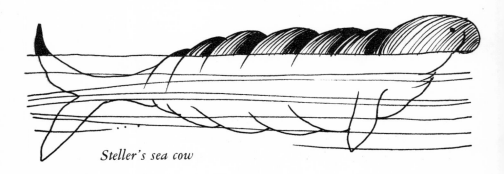

*Steller's sea cow*

One of the sea-monster carcasses that scientists argued about turned out to be a huge kind of sea cow called Steller's sea cow. But it was so tame and trusting that meat hunters killed the whole species and it became extinct soon after it was discovered. The elusive monster isn't like that!

Could Nessie be a fish?

One kind of fish, an oarfish, grows to be about 20 feet long. Some sea-serpent sightings have turned out to be oarfish. But no one has even seen an oarfish anyplace but in the deep ocean.

*oarfish*

Could the Monster be a basking shark?

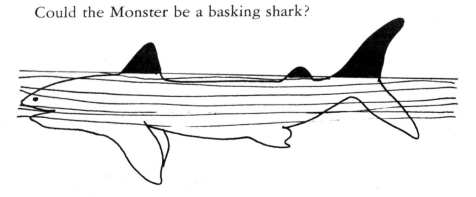

"Sea monster" skeletons that have been washed ashore on islands around Scotland have turned out to be basking sharks. The Stronsa monster was one of those. But how could sharks stay in the loch without being seen or caught? And how could they come ashore?

Some of the most detailed descriptions have been by people who watched the Monster while it was on shore, for a number of minutes. No fish could roam around at the edge of the loch.

Could Nessie be another kind of fish—maybe a giant eel?

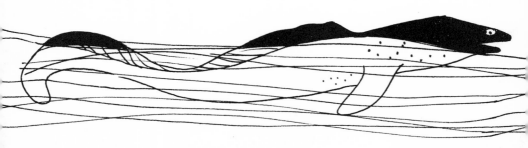

There are very big eels in the loch. One story tells about a local farmer who caught an eel so big that he needed his biggest cart to take it home. (But that may be a fish story.)

The larvae, or young, of some deep-sea eels have been reported as being almost 6 feet (close to two meters) long, which means that the adults must be enormous, maybe more than 50 feet (15.2 meters). Eel larvae leave the sea and come up rivers into fresh water to grow up, so some eel larvae could come through the canals into the lochs without being seen.

*eel larvae*

But adult eels return to the sea to spawn. Giant eels could not get back through the locks without being seen. Could there be eels that are adapted to live their whole life cycle in the lochs?

A giant eel seems a good candidate for being the Monster. Except for coming ashore. And one other thing.

Almost always, eels and other fish, snakes and other reptiles move through the water by wiggling their bodies from side to side.

Only mammals move their bodies through the water up and down.

Investigators who favor the idea that Nessie is a giant eel say that sometimes eels have been observed to swim on their sides. But when they do, they can't lift their heads the way the Monster seems to do.

Could Nessie be an amphibian?

Once there were many amphibians on earth. They were the link between fishes and reptiles. Now there are only a few—frogs and toads, newts and salamanders, and some wormlike, legless amphibians called *caecilians*.

Some descriptions of the animal in Loch Ness say that it looks like a giant newt or salamander. The shape is about right, except that the neck is too short. And some newts have a crest that looks like a mane.

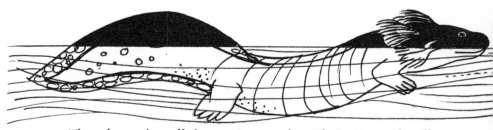

*The salamander called a mudpuppy has "hairy" outside gills.*

The most important argument for Nessie being an amphibian is that amphibians can get oxygen from the air *and* from the water. They can get oxygen through their skins. Some people say that Nessie takes air in through the skin on its humps and stores it there until it uses it. That's why the humps seem to change size.

Not much is known about the habits of the wormlike amphibians called caecilians, but some monster hunters cast their vote for them.

Could Nessie be some kind of giant worm?

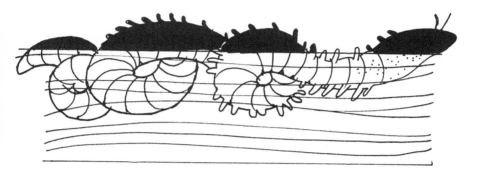

The legends tell about an animal called the Great Orm. There are carvings of it in many places. One carving was found on a stone near Urquhart Castle. The Great Orm looks very wormlike.

*The Great Orm.*

Some of the animals in Olaus Magnus's maps were giant worms. They look like descriptions of Nessie. Some worms are very, very long, but no worm has ever been known that is big around. And Nessie seems to have a thick body.

If the Loch Ness Monster *is* some kind of invertebrate—an animal without bones—that would explain why no bones have ever been found.

A squid is another invertebrate animal and there are some giants. But squids don't swim fast or act the way the animal in Loch Ness does.

Could Nessie be a giant sea slug?

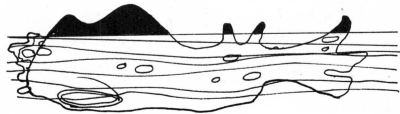

A sea slug has a soft body that could shape into humps. It breathes through gills. Sea slugs are relatives of land snails and garden slugs, which have "horns." More than one witness has compared Nessie with a snail.

But all known sea slugs live only in salt water. They never come ashore. And they eat plants. There are no growing plants in the loch, except in shallow water.

Could Nessie be not a living thing at all?

Some people say that it is

—floating leaves or logs;

—a dirigible that somehow fell into the loch during World War I and which surfaces every now and then;

—a string of buoys;

—an optical illusion made by waves on the loch.

Some people say that it's ordinary animals—otters, ducks, swimming deer.

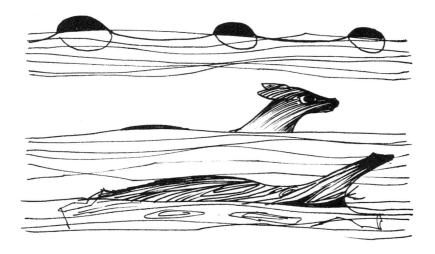

THE LOCH NESS MONSTER

*Mansell Collection*

Some people say that it's all imagination. People think they see what they want to see.

Some people say that it's all a hoax to bring tourists to Loch Ness. And there have been hoaxes. People have made fake monsters and fake monster footprints.

Most scientists say that so far there is no proof that the monster really exists.

What do you think?
Is there a real Loch Ness Monster?
What is it?

And if it's *not* real, what have so many people seen in Loch Ness?

These last few pages are reserved for when you finally find out what the Monster looks like, and what it is. Use these pages for its photograph and the news story.

# Bibliography

Adamnan, St., Reeves, William, Ed. *The Life of Saint Columba.* New York: AMS Press, Inc., 1857.

Baumann, Elwood. *The Loch Ness Monster.* New York: Franklin Watts, 1972.

Beiser, Arthur. *The Earth.* (Life Nature Library) New York: Time-Life Books, 1968.

Buchsbaum, Ralph. *Animals Without Backbones.* Chicago: University of Chicago Press, 1948.

Burton, Maurice. *The Problem of Loch Ness.* Illustrated London News

Campbell, Elizabeth Montgomery, and Solomon, David. *The Search for Morag.* New York: Walker and Company, 1973.

Colbert, Edwin. *The Age of Reptiles.* New York: E. P.
Dutton & Co., 1966.

―――*The Dinosaur Book.* New York: McGraw-Hill,
1951.

―――*Wandering Lands and Animals.* New York: E. P.
Dutton & Co., Inc., 1973.

Cohen, Daniel. *A Modern Look at Monsters.* New York:
Dodd, Mead & Company, 1970.

Costello, Peter. *In Search of Lake Monsters.* New
York: Berkley Publishing Corp., 1975.

Dinsdale, Tim. *The Loch Ness Monster,* 2nd ed. Boston:
Routledge & Kegan, 1972.

Gould, Rupert. *The Case for the Sea Serpent.* Detroit:
Gale Research Company, 1972.

Heuvelmans, Bernard. *In the Wake of the Sea Serpents.*
New York: Hill & Wang, 1968.

―――*On the Track of Unknown Animals.* Cambridge:
The M.I.T. Press, 1972.

Hickman, Hickman, and Hickman. *Integrated Principles
of Zoology.* St. Louis: The C. V. Mosby Company, 1974.

Holiday, F. W. *The Great Orm of Loch Ness.* New York:
W. W. Norton & Company, Inc., 1969.

Klein, Rines, Dinsdale, and Foster. *Underwater Search
At Loch Ness.* Boston: Academy of Applied Science,
1972.

LaPorte, L. F. *Ancient Environments.* New York:
Prentice-Hall, Inc., 1968.

Mackal, Roy, P. *The Monsters of Loch Ness.* Chicago: The
Swallow Press, Inc., 1976.

Sanderson, Ivan. *Investigating the Unexplained: A Compendium of Disquieting Mysteries of the Natural World.* New Jersey: Prentice-Hall, Inc., 1972.

Spectorsky, A. C. *Book of the Sea.* New York: Appleton-Century-Crofts, 1954.

Spinar, Z. V. *Life Before Man.* New York: McGraw-Hill, 1972.

Swinton, W. E. *Fossil Amphibians and Reptiles.* The British Natural History Museum.

Technology Review (MIT). *Search for the Loch Ness Monster.* March/April, 1976.

White, T. H. *Bestiary: A Book of Beasts.* New York: G. P. Putnam's Sons, 1960.

Whyte, Constance. *More Than A Legend.* London: Hamish Hamilton, Ltd., 1957.

Witchell, Nicholas. *The Loch Ness Story.* New York: British Book Centre, Inc., 1976.

# Index

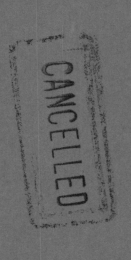